NO GREATER FRIEND

NO GREATER FRIEND

A Tribute to Dogs
and
the Owners Who Love Them

Published in the United States of America by

LMS Worldwide
Fort Wayne, IN 46804
www.lmsww.com

Copyright © 2004 by Elizabeth Lea Schatzlein
All rights reserved under International and Pan-American Copyright Conventions.
No part of this book may be reproduced, scanned, or
distributed in any printed or electronic form without permission. Please
do not participate in or encourage piracy of copyrighted materials in
violation of the author's rights. Purchase only authorized editions.

Library of Congress Cataloging-in-Publication Data
Schatzlein, Liz.
No Greater Friend / Liz Schatzlein.
p. cm.
ISBN 0-9727301-0-9
1. Dogs-Nonfiction. 2. United States. Fort Wayne, Indiana. I. Title.
2004
Printed in the United States of America 1 3 5 7 9 10 8 6 4 2
Book design by Craftline

Dedicated
To Max

1987-2002

Photo Courtesy of Liz Schatzlein

Dogs are not our whole lives
But they make our lives whole -

Roger Caras

FORWARD

Just by glancing at the cover of this book, it becomes obvious that Liz Schatzlein is a person of compassion who dearly loves dogs and people. Better than any other book I have seen, Liz has captured and demonstrated the significance of the human-companion animal bond.

As you read this book, your heart will be touched. If you have never owned a dog, you will soon realize that you cannot put a price tag upon that which you have missed.

Unlike man, our canine friends continually demonstrate unconditional, nonjudgmental love. Rather than criticize, they eagerly accept us for who we are, regardless of our current emotional state. The dog, more than any other animal or person, demonstrates best the unconditional love of God. Could this explain why the dog is considered "man's best friend" here on earth? Is it merely coincidental that dog spelled backwards is god?

Research studies demonstrate that pets produce very positive human health effects on biological, psychological, and social levels. Dogs are safe recipients of our affection who rarely, if ever, reject us. As some of the featured dogs in this book portray, they are like children; they serve as social lubricants facilitating interaction among adults, while often acting as peacemakers and tension-breakers. They entertain us, make us laugh, make us feel important and needed, give the lonely senior citizens a reason for living, and are great listeners.

Dogs are just good medicine. Touch is so important to our emotional and physical health and dogs provide that physical contact. Blood pressures of pet owners decrease when holding and stroking their furry friend. In fact, people with pets have been found to have lower triglyceride and cholesterol levels, even when compared for weight, diet, and smoking. Owning a pet not only decreases the risk of having a heart attack, but actually increases the length of time heart attack victims live after their attack.

Each year more dogs become involved in pet therapy programs for the mentally, emotionally, and terminally ill. They are also extremely productive in nursing homes and rehabilitation hospitals.

The human-animal bond becomes dramatically obvious in the case of Leader Dogs for the Blind and Canine Companions, which provides service and hearing dogs. For the person who once had to rely on others to open doors and pick up the things he or she dropped, now the service dog provides independence. For the deaf person for whom a knock on the door or a smoke alarm's warning went unheard, now the hearing dog alerts its partner to the sound.

There are occasions when dogs benefit their fellow kind along with mankind. While our Shih Tzu named Bentley James acts as the official public relations "director" at our veterinary hospital, our hospital mascot named Sizzler makes a larger sacrifice. Sizzler, whom we adopted from a Greyhound rescue organization, proved to have a universal blood type which can be given to any dog. Over the past ten years, she has helped save the lives of many dogs in desperate need of an emergency blood transfusion. She donates willingly as she looks forward to our canine version of "Thanksgiving" dinner which follows.

As a veterinarian, I witness daily how pets enrich people's lives. At the same time, I watch pet owners repeatedly make major sacrifices for their animal family members. This book is not only a tribute to dogs, but to their dedicated caring owners who daily fulfill Proverbs 12:10, "A righteous man cares for the needs of his animal."

Thank you Liz for further revealing the life-giving significance of the human-animal bond. As we walk through the inevitable tough times here on earth, it is comforting to have our faithful canine companion at our side to remind us that we have "no greater friend."

Dr. Dan Rodgers

Dr. Dan Rodgers and his wife Tammy with their Greyhound, Sizzler and Shih Tzu, Bentley.

AN EXPLANATION AND SOME THANKS FROM THE AUTHOR

This book has been 20 years in the making, eighteen-and-a-half years just thinking about it, one-and-a-half years actually working on it. It was almost two years ago over lunch with my good friend Carol Tanner that I first tentatively voiced my desire to do a book about dogs and their owners. I was braced for roars of laughter, but instead, Carol offered to buy the first copy. Dog lover that she is, she thought it was a wonderful idea. That was the boost my confidence needed, and I was officially off and running.

The idea for the book began in the early 1980s, when I was an anchor for WANE-TV, the CBS affiliate in Fort Wayne, Indiana. I was assigned to cover a house fire, which seemed pretty standard. What wasn't standard was how the fire started. In an unbelievable act of cruelty, two juveniles had poured gasoline over a puppy and set her ablaze. Terrified, the puppy, named Sheba, ran into a house and under a chair. She set the chair on fire, which subsequently started the house fire. Sheba survived, but was horribly burned. She was taken to the St. Joe Center Veterinary Hospital, where she stayed for many months as they worked first to save her life, then to rehabilitate her.

It was mind-boggling that someone would harm an innocent animal in this way, but what happened next was even more incredible. The television station was swamped with calls and letters from people who wanted to take Sheba. The Department of Animal Control was inundated with requests to give Sheba a new home. Hundreds of people expressed interest. The evil that had caused Sheba's injuries was dwarfed by the outpouring of love from the community. It seemed everybody wanted this dog!

It was finally decided to give Sheba to the Emergency Medical Technician who had pulled her out of the fire. The day Sheba was finally released to go to her new home the news media was there in full. As the badly scarred little dog ran to meet her new owner, I watched hard-nosed news photographers who were known to eat cheeseburgers at the scene of fatal car accidents wipe away tears. It was a horrific tale with a very happy ending, and to this day is the favorite story of my career. Sheba had done something that is hard to do - she had genuinely touched hearts.

Animals, dogs in particular, seem to have a way of doing that. It can be difficult to get people to open up about themselves, but ask them about their dog and there's no quieting them. According to the United States Census Bureau, nearly 36-percent of American homes include at least one dog. That's a lot of canine companions.

A professor I had at Purdue once told me that the first items people buy when setting up a house are electronics, televisions and the like. With apologies to this particular prof, he didn't understand dog lovers. When my stepdaughter, Tricia, was in law school at Duke University and got her first apartment, one of her first purchases was a beautiful Golden Retriever she named Indiana. She got her dog even before she bought a DVD player! Indiana is now a beloved member in the home she shares with her husband, Andy Smock.

Our own home boasts no less than four Pugs, named Thing, Beulah, Liddy and Kiwi, and I can't imagine our lives without them. There's a lot of dog hair to clean up, and a lot of barking and snorting to tolerate (not to mention Pug snoring, something that has to be heard to be believed), but they are family and we love them dearly.

I knew there were many stories like Sheba's out there, perhaps not as dramatic, but just as poignant. I only wish I had the time and the room to tell all of them. As it is, I narrowed the list to twenty-two. Some of the folks profiled are good friends of mine, some were recommended to me and some called me personally to tell me about their dog and why they needed to be in the book!

They all have something in common - they are exceptional people who love their dogs very much. It has been a joy to get to know them, and an honor to share their stories.

"Thank you's" are a must - writing a book isn't as easy as I thought it would be and I couldn't have done it without the help and support of many people.

First and foremost, I am forever indebted to Lori Hunt, a gifted photographer who shared my vision for this work. Lori toiled tirelessly for over a year on this project, and took some truly beautiful pictures. This was her first time photographing animals, no small challenge, but she visually captured the special relationships detailed in the narrative. She also developed a pretty wicked dog whistle in the process, which caught the attention of dogs and owners alike during every photo session!

I would also like to thank Dr. Dan Rodgers of the Aboite Animal Hospital, one of the best veterinarians in Fort Wayne, Indiana and a great help in putting this book together.

Thank you also to my dear friend Kris Rajchel, who read the draft of this book, and then read it again, to make sure everything made sense.

Others who deserve a pat on the back for their support and assistance include Carol Tanner, Lisa Fabian, Marcia Holland, Lauren Holloway (for the cute Pug tote - very handy when writing a book!), my personal trainer Pam Holt (for helping me keep the faith), Andy Candor, the staff at Visiting Nurse and Hospice Home, the Asher Agency, Bruce Boxberger (for making sure all my legal t's were crossed), Alice Robinson, Julie Roach at Craftline Printing, Tiffy Joy, my parents, Robert Berry and Martina Perella, and my brother Steve Berry.

And of course, my wonderful husband, Mike, who bought me my very first pug, Max, 16 years ago and never wavered in his support for this project, and my incredible son, Derek, who is the light of my life and helped me tremendously through this endeavor. Your support and love mean more to me than anything. Thank you for believing.

Derek, Mike and Liz Schatzlein with their pack of Pugs, Beulah, Liddy, Kiwi and Thing.

The one absolutely unselfish friend that man can have in this selfish world, the one that never deserts him, the one that never proves ungrateful or treacherous, is his dog.

George Graham Vest

DUMPSTER DOG

There are rough starts in life, and then there are rough starts in life. In November 1998, things were looking pretty bleak for one particular five-week-old yellow Labrador Retriever. Along with his seven littermates, he had been stuffed into a plastic garbage bag and tossed into an apartment complex dumpster, left to die by a heartless owner. A terrible fate, but luck was on this litter's side. The puppies were cold, hungry and scared, and were making quite a bit of racket down in that dumpster. A passerby heard their whimpering, dug them out of the dumpster, and promptly set about finding them homes. He had found homes for all but one, the runt, when he contacted schoolteacher Carol Israel's daughter. She already had a dog, but she thought her mother might be able to help. She took the puppy to her mother's elementary school, to see if Carol could find him a home.

Carol showed the puppy to everyone during the day, but her efforts quickly became half-hearted. "The more people looked at the puppy, the more I didn't want them to take him," says Carol. She was hooked. By the end of the day, Carol had taken her "dumpster dog" to meet her then-fiancé, Charlie Steinbrecher, and Charlie was sold. The three of them have been together ever since. They named the puppy Indiana, and according to Carol, he bears no emotional scars from his cruel beginnings. She says Indiana is the best dog, loving, playful and loyal. Carol says at least once a week, she and Charlie look at each other and say, "Can you believe this dog was supposed to die?" If you mention to her how lucky Indiana is, however, Carol will quickly correct you. "Nope," she says with a smile, "we're the lucky ones."

Carol Israel and Charlie Steinbrecher with Indiana, a very lucky yellow Labrador.

JUST GIMME SOME KIND OF SIGN

It started with one simple command, "sit." That single directive blossomed into a vast repertoire of commands that little Midnight the Poodle can perform at the wave of a hand - or the point of a finger or two. Thanks to owner Carol Hupp, Midnight knows sign language, the language of the hearing-impaired. Carol, who volunteers in the hearing-impaired classrooms at Harris Elementary School, started teaching the two-year-old Poodle the special language when she was only eight weeks old. "She was a very quick study," says Carol, who has now taught Midnight more complex commands, including "go get in your bed" and "wipe your feet!"

While Midnight easily steals the show at cocktail parties, Carol had a much more serious task in mind. Midnight occasionally tags along when Carol goes to Harris Elementary, delighting the hearing-impaired students Carol teaches. Closely watching the rapidly moving hands of the children, Midnight faithfully carries out whatever commands they give her. For many students, it is the first time they've been able to communicate with a dog, and according to Carol, "it just brings tears to your eyes." It's a wonderful experience for the children, and a terrific time for Midnight, who thoroughly enjoys the interaction. "Everyone loves her," says Carol. Having the hearing-impaired children communicate with a dog has been a dream of Carol's, a dream that Midnight made a reality. "Poodles are so smart," she says. In sign language, or any language, that means "Good job, Midnight!"

Midnight the Poodle waits anxiously for her next sign language command from owner Carol Hupp.

JUSTICE PREVAILS

It's not unusual for a police officer to feel close to his partner. Officer Gary Howard will always have a special feeling for his partner, who has come between him and danger more than once. "There's no doubt he's saved my life," says Howard, a member of the Fort Wayne Police Department. "Most people see him and don't want to fight." That's because Gary Howard's partner is a five-year-old Dutch Shepherd dog, appropriately named Officer Justice. Justice was born and bred in Holland, a country known for turning out fine police dogs. Gary learned Dutch, so he could give Justice his commands in a language the dog understood.

In their years together, the two partners have been through it all, and have grown to trust and depend on one another. According to Gary, "a suspect assumes a different attitude" when he sees Justice coming at him. Gary recalls how Justice helped him catch a criminal who was fleeing the scene. "The suspect took off running," he says, "so I released the dog." When Gary caught up with the suspect, he found Justice already had him cornered, and Gary was sure the man wasn't going anywhere. "Justice was standing there like a stone, with his nose pushed into the guy's crotch. That guy was literally in a cold sweat." The dog had made his point, so to speak. Justice had convinced the suspect that running wasn't in his best interest, and Gary said the man was actually relieved to be arrested.

As taxing as police work is, life is not "all work and no play." K-9 officers live with their partners, and off the job, Gary says Justice is just like any other family pet, very much the baby. He loves to play in the water and he loves to fetch. Justice is a wonderful pet, and an exemplary police officer, especially when it comes to trustworthiness. "I left a hamburger and fries in the squad car one day," Gary says, "when I got back, Justice was staring at the burger sack, but he hadn't touched it." Now that's a partner you've got to love.

Fort Wayne City Police Officer Gary Howard with Officer Justice, a member of the K-9 squad.

ENDLESS NIGHT

The lights went out for Harley when he was two years old. "You could just tell something was wrong," says endodontist Dr. Todd Mabry, who had begun to notice his black Labrador Retriever hunting dog was having vision problems. Before long, his worst fears were confirmed - Harley was suffering from retinal degeneration. Within a short time, he was completely blind. "We're seeing it more in this breed," Todd says, mostly due to inbreeding. The condition is permanent. There is no cure.

So what do you do with a hunting dog that has lost his sight? Well, if you're Todd Mabry, you take him right back out in the field. Harley, now seven-years-old, hasn't let his handicap slow him down. Harley still does what he was bred to do - retrieve prey. According to Todd, he does it very well. Harley has learned to adapt. "He high-steps," explains Todd, meaning that Harley lifts his front feet far off the ground when he walks so he can negotiate the terrain. And the black Lab's nose works overtime, to guide him through woods and fields. It's not an ideal situation - Harley still bumps into the occasional tree - but he can find ducks and pheasants when Todd and his 15-year-old son Ryan go hunting. At home, Harley reverts to beloved family pet. "Yeah, he's a big baby," says Ryan.

As adept as Harley has become at getting around, Todd still keeps a watchful eye on him. But get rid of him? Never. As Todd will tell you with big grin, sight or no sight, "Harley is a great dog!"

Dr. Todd Mabry and his son Ryan take a break with Harley, the blind hunting dog.

THE MORE, THE MERRIER!

Television journalist Jennifer Blomquist has never met a dog she didn't like. She's also never met one she didn't want to take home. That's why you'll find Sophie, J.J. and Wrigley playing couch potato on her sofa. All three dogs were homeless when the 21Alive news anchor found them, and "just say no" wasn't in her vocabulary.

Sophie the Beagle mix came first, in 1996. "She was so sweet," says Jennifer, who took Sophie after her owner dropped her off at the SPCA. Just six weeks later Sophie was joined by J.J., a Labrador puppy who also needed a home. Jennifer's boyfriend at the time (now her husband), Mark Gidley, did his best to try to talk her out of dog number three, but his arguments fell on deaf ears. "I just wanted the dog," she says, and so Wrigley, another orphan pooch, joined the fast-growing Blomquist pack. Mark wasn't initially thrilled with the whole canine clan, but Jennifer and the dogs were definitely a package deal. "He just had to get over that," laughs Jennifer, who is happy to report they are all now one big, happy family. "Mark has bonded with them," she says, especially J.J., who was diagnosed with epilepsy and had to undergo treatment at the Purdue Small Animal Hospital, a time consuming and costly endeavor.

The arrival of twin sons Matthew and Luke in 2003 changed the dynamics of the house, but it's all good. The dogs seem to be hitting it off with the twins, and the babies are even bringing out Sophie's maternal instincts. "She'll sit between the boys on the floor," says Jennifer, "she's very protective." Sophie isn't the only one who's protective. Jennifer sighs and shakes her head, "I just can't understand people who abuse animals. I could never hurt a dog." Although the twins have put a lid on any more dog adoptions for now, their big-hearted Mom will never say never. At Jennifer's house, there will always be room for one more.

Jennifer Blomquist surrounded by those who mean the most to her – husband Mark Gidley, twin sons Matthew and Luke, and canine crew Wrigley, J.J. and Sophie.

A BULLDOG BABE AND A LUSCIOUS LAB: IRMSCHER'S ANGELS

"We've made a lot of friends by having the dogs," Mox Irmscher says with a grin. It's no wonder. There's just something about seeing a 35-pound Bulldog lumbering toward you sporting a bridal veil that makes people want to come up and say "hi," or at least "what the heck?"

And plenty of people notice Mox and Lisa Irmscher's dogs. It's hard not to. On any given day, Stinky, the seven-year-old Bulldog, and Vivian, a seven-year-old yellow Labrador, will greet you at the door in a variety of get-ups that would make even the Hilton sisters green with envy. Stinky can be stunning as a princess, while Vivian dazzles as a daffodil. Or Stinky might don a fetching bumblebee ensemble, while Vivian opts for a Fourth-of-July "Uncle Sam" look. "For Halloween, we disguised them as Dalmatians," deadpans Mox. "They're our babies," laughs Lisa, who enjoys scouting out the very best in canine couture. But no regular doggie duds will do for these two gals. "I shop in children's departments," says Lisa, who outfits Stinky and Vivian in prêt-a-porter bonnets, necklaces and matching wardrobe pieces.

While it's obviously all in good fun, there is no doubt about the very special place the two dogs have in the household. These are two well-loved - and pampered - pups. The Irmschers took a room in their home and turned it over to the dogs, outfitting it with dog beds, dog-sized furniture, and yes, fire hydrants.

They even hired an artist from Michigan to do murals on the wall (of Stinky and Vivian, of course). Professional photographs of Stinky and Vivian in various attire abound in the house ("these dogs are gonna break me," jokes Mox). The dogs love the attention, and everyone seems to love Stinky and Vivian. "They are picture perfect pets," says Lisa. And they are always ready for their close-ups.

Mox and Lisa Irmscher relax with Stinky, wearing her favorite bonnet, and Vivian, in her daisy collar, in the dogs' special room, complete with hand-painted wall mural.

SAVING MISS SADIE

I f Sadie were a cat, she would be on life number nine right now. Fortunately for her, Sadie is a dog, owned by two people who would move heaven and earth before they would let anything happen to her. Page and Nicole Hoover have been through the mill with the nine-year-old Greyhound, enduring ordeals that would cause other people to walk away. Not the Hoovers. "We love her," says Nicole, who still tears up as she tells the story of Sadie's extremely close call. The Hoovers adopted Sadie in 1996 through Greyhound Companions, an organization that finds homes for the racing dogs when their careers come to an end. Little did they know what was in store. "If it can happen, it happens to Sadie," says Nicole. While taking their afternoon stroll one day, Sadie was attacked by a Labrador, who took a huge chunk out of Sadie's flank. She survived that attack, but the worst was yet to come.

It was October of 2001, and Page remembers it all happened rather quickly. Sadie went from healthy and happy to lethargic within the course of a day. She was vomiting and she wouldn't eat. "She just wasn't herself," he says, "something was very wrong." A trip to the veterinarian's office explained why. It turns out Sadie was in full kidney failure, close to death. She was shipped down to the Purdue Small Animal Hospital in West Lafayette, Indiana, where she spent three weeks in intensive care. The diagnosis: leptospirosis, life-threatening bacteria that are spread through urine. Page thinks Sadie must have been exposed while she was walking on the golf course behind their house.

Sadie dwindled from 70 to 47 pounds. The veterinarians at Purdue prepared Hoovers for the worst. The prognosis was not good. Devastated, Page and Nicole commuted daily from Fort Wayne to West Lafayette to see Sadie, even if it was only for a few minutes at a time. They weren't ready to say goodbye, but as it turns out, Sadie wasn't ready to leave. Against all odds and surprising nearly everyone, Sadie pulled through, eventually able to return home, although she needed a feeding tube for the next two-and-a-half months. This Greyhound won the race of her life, and should any more "races" come up, Sadie needn't worry. The Hoovers will be right there, to go the distance with her.

Page and Nicole Hoover with Sadie, their rescued Greyhound.

HOW TO MEND A BROKEN HEART

L ife is uncertain. We never know what lies just around the corner. No one knows that lesson better than Lynne Gilmore. For Lynne, great happiness came from unbearable sorrow. In the summer of 2001, Lynne and her husband Mark were preparing for the adoption of the baby they had always wanted. They had waited a long time to take that step, and now that the decision was made, both were eager to welcome the new addition to the family. But life took a cruel twist. That July, without warning, Lynne suffered a near fatal heart attack, resulting in an emergency angioplasty. As Lynne struggled to recuperate, the adoption was canceled. It was a double blow - not only did she have a life-threatening heart condition, but her dreams of motherhood were gone. It was a dark time.

Six months after her heart attack, Lynne knew she "needed something to nurture." And she knew just what she needed - a puppy. Her love found a willing recipient in a frisky, white-haired bundle of energy that Mark named Tiger. The four-month-old Lhasa Apso proved to be just the bright spot that both Gilmores needed. Instead of dwelling on the negative things that had happened, Lynne could now dote on their new family member, who made himself right at home! Not only did Tiger readily accept all the affection Lynne and Mark could shower on him, but in typical canine-style, he returned that love.

Now the couple can't remember what their home was like before the little whirlwind arrived. Lynne makes Tiger's food from scratch (he's partial to omelettes), and Mark, who was at first skeptical about getting the dog, is now Tiger's biggest fan. In fact, the Gilmore's were so happy with Tiger that they recently added one more. Tiger now has a Lhasa Apso sister named Lily. There is no doubt that Tiger helped get Lynne through the most difficult time of her life. "My heart is happy," she sighs.

Tiger takes his rightful place front and center with his Mom and Dad, Lynne and Mark Gilmore.

TO THE RESCUE

Jill Burnett is making up for lost time. During her childhood she was so desperate for a dog, she says, she "used to keep a cat on a leash." No more. The young girl who was denied a dog as a child has become the rescuer of countless abused and unwanted dogs. Today no less than four dogs call this Canterbury School science teacher's house home. They include 18-and-a-half year old Michie, who suffers from vertigo, a Beagle named Hillary, a mutt called BOO Myer, and S.P. i C.A., a Norwegian Elk Hound/Border Collie mix who gets his name from the place Jill found him, the Society for the Prevention of Cruelty to Animals, or SPCA. Jill added the "i" to make it pronounceable. A fifth dog, her beloved mixed breed L.B., recently had to be euthanized, an episode that was profoundly painful for Jill.

All Jill's dogs were in need of a good home when she found them, but BOO Myer (the "Myer" is in honor of her father, the "BOO" comes from the dog's intense fear of people) has probably the saddest tale to tell. Mercilessly abused before being adopted by Jill, it took BOO Myer well over five years of tender loving care to be even somewhat comfortable around people. "The dog was a real mess," says Jill, who is proud of the progress BOO Myer has made.

If Jill can't take a dog herself, she pounds the pavement until she finds someone who can, as many of her friends and acquaintances can attest. "My goal every year is to find homes for at least two dogs," she says. If there's a dog in need, Jill will answer the call. "I just couldn't imagine not having a dog," she says. The pooches who share her life hope she never will. Jill's home is truly their safe harbor.

Jill Burnett poses with her clan, Michie, S.P.i C.A, Boo Myer, and Hillary.

TWIN SONS OF DIFFERENT MOTHERS

To the casual observer, Golden Retrievers Bailey and James look nearly identical. But to owner Sandi Kemmish, they are as different as night and day. Bailey, the younger dog, is energetic and playful. James, at 12 years old, is more laid-back. "His heart beats once a month," jokes Sandi. While the bond between owner and dog can be strong, so can the bond between two individual dogs. That's what happened with Bailey and James. Sandi and her husband, Kirk, owned another Golden Retriever years ago - James' mother. When that dog passed away, James, six years old at the time, was grief-stricken. Puppy Bailey arrived not long after and, far from resenting the new dog, Sandi says Bailey actually helped James get over the death of his mother. James needed another canine companion, and Bailey filled the role.

The two dogs are inseparable, even if James has a tough time now keeping up with the rowdy Bailey. Bailey loves to play water frisbee at Kemmish's lake cottage. Just don't expect him to play fair. "He won't give you back the frisbee," says Sandi, who adds Bailey isn't really into sharing his lake toys. James likes to take an occasional dip in the water, too, but you had best be up on your lifesaving skills. Poor James jumped in a pond once and promptly sank, forcing Sandi to dive in and save him.

The Kemmish's have owned other breeds in the past, including Irish Setters, Gordon Setters and a Siberian Husky, but the Goldens, according to Sandi, have been wonderful pets. She echoes what many dog owners feel. "They give you unconditional love," says Sandi, "they don't care how bad the day has been or what kind of mood you're in. They just love you." Bailey and James are true friends, to each other and their owner. It's just hard to say goodbye. That's the problem with man's best friends, says Sandi, "They don't live long enough."

Sandi Kemmish flanked by her Golden Retriever boys, Bailey and James.

WILD BOARS BEWARE!

When Bruce and Vickie Boxberger decided to get a dog, they considered many of the breeds found on the official American Kennel Club list. What they ended up getting is a breed not many people have heard of and even fewer can pronounce. Their little white dog, Topanga, is often mistaken for a Shih Tzu or a Lhasa Apso, but she is neither one. Topanga is a Coton DeTulear (pronounced coe-TAWN day TULE-ee-r), a breed not well known in this country and not officially recognized by the AKC. Vickie says Coton owners want to keep it that way, to maintain control of this very special little dog.

Don't be fooled by their small stature. According to Vickie, Cotons are considered the "Royal Dogs of Madagascar," and were originally bred to chase mice and rats and hunt wild boar. Difficult imagery to be sure, but apparently looks can be deceiving. These little white fur balls were very good at their jobs, and were positively revered in their home country. Those chasing and hunting instincts continue today, and while Topanga doesn't get the opportunity to chase rats in Fort Wayne (much less wild boar), she's not opposed to racing a visiting dog, or human, around Bruce and Vickie's backyard.

Topanga arrived at the Fort Wayne International Airport from the state of Washington on Halloween night, 1998, and the Boxberger's daughter Melissa promptly named her after a favorite television character. The family, who had previously owned a rather laid-back Poodle, had to acclimate themselves to their new feisty member. "She's almost cat-like the way she climbs furniture," says Vickie, who for that reason is thankful the breed doesn't shed much. She has filled a void in Bruce and Vickie's lives, empty nesters now who miss not having someone to nurture. But Cotons are not for the energetically-impaired. "She makes us feel younger," says Vickie, "because she's always running around the house! She's never still!" She keeps Bruce and Vickie on their toes. And if by some chance a wild boar should happen to wander into Boxberger's yard, Topanga's got them covered there, too!

Topanga shares a rare quiet moment with owners Bruce and Vickie Boxberger.

THE BIRTHDAY BUDDY

R ichard Hoying's 41st birthday won't be one he will soon forget. His friends made sure of that. Richard, the general manager at Jorgensen's, an upscale gift store, was a dog sitter in his spare time, taking care of his friends' dogs when they left town. He, however, had remained "dogless" for his entire adult life. That was about to change.

Seven of those friends thought it was high time Richard had a pet to call his own. They banded together and surprised Richard with his very own miniature Dachshund, the kind of dog Richard's family had owned when he was growing up. Once the shock wore off, it didn't take long for the dog to endear himself to Richard, even though Richard says people often confused the puppy with a ferret.

The biggest challenge of instant fatherhood was coming up with a name for the little guy. Richard hit the Internet, searching Dachshund websites for the perfect German name. In the end, fancy names were tossed aside. "Buddy" seemed the perfect choice, since he had been a gift from all of Richard's buddies.

Richard and Buddy are now inseparable, and Jorgensen's customers have lavished "shower" gifts on the young Dachshund, including his own three-piece set of red luggage. Buddy has also brought out Richard's more nurturing - and patient - side. He indulges Buddy's refusal to eat green Fruit Loops ("he eats every other color," Richard sighs). And Buddy seems to be changing the priorities of the household. Richard used to blanch white and break out in a cold sweat if someone tracked mud in his house, but he's learning to be more relaxed. "Once you've seen your dog pee on your expensive Oriental rug," he jokes, "you just go with it."

Buddy will soon get a chance to use his luggage set - Richard has decided to resume dog sitting. Buddy, of course, will be going along. Who knew that a tiny, green-Fruit-Loop-hatin' wiener dog could add so much to life? Seven good friends did. Happy Birthday, Richard!

Richard Hoying with his best buddy, Buddy.

BIKER BOY

Sometimes in life, we get a second chance. One night at a charity auction, Jim Bailey and his wife Marcia spotted a beautiful Golden Retriever puppy that was up for bid. "We just fell in love with him," says Jim, "we wanted him bad that night." It wasn't to be. The dog went to another bidder, and the Harley-Davidson dealership owner and his wife went home, empty-handed and dejected. But they didn't stay down for long. Within days they got a call from the new owner, who was suffering with allergy-related sneezing and sniffling caused by the puppy. Would the Baileys still be interested in taking him? No question about it.

Just like that, Gordy the Golden Retriever had a new home, and Jim and Marcia found their collective world turned upside down. "I get too emotional, I can't leave the dog," explains Jim. So Gordy comes to work with Jim and Marcia every day, romping and playing in their store, all 60,000 square feet of it. Gordy loves to run on the smooth floors, although "stopping is still a problem," Jim says with a straight face. Naturally, he's made friends with the customers. "They don't come to see us," Jim says, "they come to see the dog."

Jim and Marcia had been thinking about getting a dog for ten years, but they travel frequently for business and didn't know how they would manage. With Gordy, though, they have happily made the adjustment. Now, if they can't take Gordy with them when they leave, one of them stays home. "He's already gotten me out of two dealer shows this month," laughs Jim, "he's totally changed our lives." Marcia says Gordy doesn't ride on the motorcycles, but he adores car trips. That's good, because with his new mom and dad, he'll be hitting the road often. "Everything we do includes him," says Jim.

Harley-Davidson store owner Jim Bailey offers a treat to Gordy, his Golden Retriever.

MIGHTY MINNIE

When you walk through Karen and Brad Springer's house, watch where you step. You may inadvertently take out the family pet. Minnie, a Chihuahua the Springers bought for their son, lives up - or down - to her name.

When the family purchased Minnie thirteen years ago as a puppy, she weighed only one-and-a-half pounds. But today, mighty Minnie tips the scales at, well, maybe two-and-a-half pounds, if she's had a really good meal and is wearing a heavy sweater. "People are always going 'is that a dog?" laughs Karen, "I forget how small she really is." So tiny is she that the Springers don't take her outside to potty. Minnie is never without her protective sweater, but still the least little breeze chills her to the bone. "Minnie uses a doggie litter box," explains Karen, who adds the little dog has been litter box trained since day one.

Minnie may be size-challenged, but don't think for one minute that she's not tough. Minnie survived a year at Indiana University in Bloomington, in a house with five rowdy guys no less. When the Springer's son, Bradley, went back to I.U. for his senior year, he decided to take little Minnie along with him. According to Karen, "she participated in a lot of I.U. parties," including a Mexican fiesta where she donned a sombrero (albeit a very tiny sombrero). Karen says the guys in the house loved her, and more importantly, so did the girls. "She was a chick magnet, they thought she was a puppy," Karen says with a grin.

No matter how good she was for their love lives, Bradley and his roommates returned Minnie to his parents after he graduated. He was headed to a job in chilly Montana, and "Minnie just can't make it in Montana. That's too much," says Karen. So she is back home - for now. Karen says her son just informed them he's coming back to Indiana to attend law school. Could there be a Doctor of Jurisprudence in Minnie's future? Stay tuned . . .

Karen Springer snuggles tiny Minnie the Chihuahua.

DISCOVERING THE HUMAN IN ALL OF US

Jeno Stabelli doesn't know he's a dog. Nobody's communicated that to him. As far as he's concerned, he is a fully functioning member of the Stabelli household - and that's just fine with his owner. It's clear when you see Joe Stabelli and Jeno together, there is a special bond.

Although he has been legally blind since birth, Joe, a retired psychotherapist, can see things many people can't, such as how to treat others with love and respect, even if they have four legs and a tail. In fact, in the Stabelli household, it's all about respect. After all, the well-behaved nine-year-old Doberman didn't get that way by accident. Joe says training a dog is a lot like counseling, you don't criticize. Instead, "the more you love them, the more they'll do," says Joe.

What you won't find Jeno doing is stupid pet tricks. It's demeaning to the dog and Joe won't have it. "You get the dog to do what he would normally do anyway," Joe says, except on command. So successful has Joe been in his training of Jeno that the two make regular rounds to area nursing homes to visit residents. Joe thinks people respond readily to Jeno because dogs touch us in a way others can't. "They help you be more human," says Joe, noting that dogs can bring out the very best in people. "They make us responsible," he says, "I feel committed to doing what I need to do for him." That means you'll find Joe walking Jeno through his neighborhood, regardless of the weather, and Jeno returns the favor by alerting Joe to obstacles that may be in his path.

Jeno, however, isn't above needing a little mommy-love if he's not feeling well. "He goes to Judy," laughs Joe, who says his wife is all too willing to show the Doberman the necessary TLC. According to Joe, that's the most successful component in an owner-dog relationship. It's what we as humans can offer a dog, says Joe, "all you have is your love."

Jeno the Doberman unwinds with owner Joe Stabelli and his granddaughter Amber Carnahan.

STAND BY ME

Sara Keltsch found love on the Internet. Not with her husband, Dan, but with her two-year-old Tibetan Terrier, Winston. After deciding it was time to get a dog, Sara surfed the net until she found a breeder in Florida who had just the dog she was looking for. But locating Winston on the world wide web proved to be much easier than getting him to Indiana. Little did Sara know what travails she and Winston would have to go through to get him to his new home in the Hoosier state.

Winston's breeder was in St. Petersburg, and Sara couldn't stand the thought of the tiny puppy flying alone in a crate to Fort Wayne. So Sara took a day off work and flew to St. Petersburg to personally retrieve Winston. The plane had no sooner landed in the Sunshine State, however, than Sara started to feel sick, really sick. Sara knew this was no case of motion sickness. Something was definitely wrong. It turns out she was having a serious gallbladder attack that doubled her over with pain. Doctors strongly recommended she stay in St. Petersburg, but Sara was determined to get Winston home.

Loaded up on pain pills, Sara boarded the plane with Winston in tow, and flew back to Fort Wayne. For Sara, it was the longest flight of her life, but Winston was good as gold for the entire trip. Sara just kept concentrating on the little puppy in her lap, and tried to ignore the searing pain in her stomach. It was a bonding experience par excellence. Once they got home, Winston stayed by her side throughout her gallbladder ordeal, helping his new Mom with her recovery. He was rewarded for his efforts - Sara admits Winston is spoiled. "People love him. And he loves the attention," she says, particularly when Mom and Winston hit the town in their matching leopard-skin coats.

Winston has also expanded Sara's business horizons. Pre-Winston, Sara didn't carry pet items in her gift store, The Monogram Shoppe. Now, she can't keep them in stock. "It's amazing what people will do for their dogs," Sara says, and she should know!

Sara Keltsch and Winston look oh-so-chic on a snowy winter morning.

HEART OF GOLDY

No one has to tell Goldy a patient is sick or dying. After four years on the job, this intuitive Golden Retriever just knows. Goldy is a therapy dog, certified by the Fort Wayne Obedience Training Club.

The six-year-old dog makes the rounds weekly at local hospitals, nursing homes and Hospice Home. It's a visit both Goldy and the patients eagerly anticipate. Handler Bob Everest says he's seen remarkable things happen when Goldy comes on the scene. Hospice patients who haven't responded to human touch will suddenly smile when Goldy nuzzles their hand. If the patient doesn't mind, Bob says Goldy "will get right up in bed with them."

Goldy's caring touch didn't happen overnight. It took hard work, for both Bob and the dog. Goldy had to go through an eight-week obedience course, then another eight-week course to learn to be a therapy dog. The training not only sensitizes the dog to the ill and the dying, but gets the dog used to a multitude of distractions that will be encountered in a typical therapy visit, such as IVs, wheelchairs and other necessary medical equipment. Toward the end of the training comes the "big night" - the dogs and their handlers spend the entire evening going up and down elevators, to get the dog used to the sensation.

Goldy works in tandem with another Golden Retriever named Akaria. Together they bring a little cheer to people who often don't have many reasons to feel happy. "The animals tune in to the people," says Bob, and without question, the patients tune in to Goldy.

Handler Bob Everest, Goldy and Akaria provide a tender moment for a patient at Visiting Nurse and Hospice Home.

A LADY IN WAITING

It had been a rough two weeks for Carol Tanner. It was March of 1999, and Carol had just put her beloved 16-year-old dog, Bandit, to sleep. Bandit's loss left an enormous void, one Carol didn't think could ever be filled - until a chance stop at the SPCA changed everything. On a whim, Carol pulled into the parking lot and went inside, where the balm to ease her pain just happened to be waiting. Carol set her eyes on an adorable German Shepherd/Collie mix pup that had been dropped off just four days earlier, and that was that. Carol knew she had found the dog. She had found Lady.

Lady didn't have time to get settled in at the SPCA, for the very next day Carol and her husband Gary brought Lady home. There's even a plaque in their garden to commemorate the day - March 20, 1999. And make no mistake, this is Lady's house now. She has her very own greeting that some might find a little uncomfortable. It's the official dog salute, taken to extremes. Anyone who enters has to pass the smell test. "When you walk in, she'll sniff you up and down," says Carol, "and when she's satisfied she'll leave you alone." Lady, however, is very thorough, and the "exam" can take awhile. Those who know Lady well know it's best to just stand still and take it; otherwise it will be a very long night.

An only child, Lady does have her very own recliner in the family room, but no spoiled brat is she. According to Carol, she lives up to her name, good-natured and even-tempered, every bit a lady, even while she's giving you the once-over with her nose. Carol says she will never forget Bandit, but Lady has brought her new joy and happiness. And the feeling apparently is mutual. Carol says when she comes through the door at night, she swears she can see Lady smile!

Carol Tanner and a smiling Lady enjoy a beautiful summer day in Lakeside Park.

DICTIONARY DIVA

Tracy and Lisa Warner have to watch what they say around the house, not because of the ears of their nine-year-old daughter, Paige, but because of their 12-year-old Border Collie, Asta. While Asta can't converse with you about the Pythagorean Theorem (yet), she does have an astonishing ability to understand English.

Tracy, the editorial page editor for the *Fort Wayne Journal Gazette*, says they really didn't think too much about Asta's comprehension skills, until a story broke about another Border Collie named Rico. The Max Planck Institute for Evolutionary Anthropology in Germany reported that Rico could understand more than 200 words, suggesting that humans aren't the only ones who can grasp the concept of language.

It was then that Tracy and Lisa started counting Asta's vocabulary and realized the dog could understand close to 100 words, even differentiating between very similar items. "She's very smart," says Tracy, who points out Border Collies are known for their intelligence. Not surprisingly, many of Asta's words are food oriented - words like pizza, treat and shrimp pop up on her vocab list. "But not those little cocktail shrimp," Tracy clarifies, "she wants the big, jumbo kind."

It was Lisa who selected Asta at the Animal Care and Control Shelter when the pup was just six weeks old. Lisa, a former dog groomer, could tell the dog was intelligent just by the look in her eyes. The Warners named her Asta, after the dog in *The Thin Man* movie series, and she quickly lived up to Lisa's expectations.

Very easy to train, the Warners used to take Asta to the park for her walk (yes, she understood the word "park" and caught on quickly when they tried spelling it instead), but no one had to bother holding the leash. Asta was only too happy to hold the end of her own leash in her mouth while they trotted along.

Arthritis has taken some of the zip out of her step, but it hasn't affected Asta's ability to understand and communicate. Fiercely protective of her family, Asta will bark serious trash at any large dog that has the misfortune of walking by the Warner home - but only after the interloper is well out of striking distance. "She waits until they get past, then she barks," laughs Tracy. Smart move on Asta's part. Just what she's saying to the other dog when she lets loose, the Warners will leave to your imagination, but they bet it isn't "shrimp."

Lisa, Paige and Tracy Warner with the incredible Asta.

A FACE EVERY MOTHER COULD LOVE

Jane Jorgensen is not prone to impulsive actions. That's why her passion for an orphan dog caught everyone by surprise, including Jane. It was a random glance at the television set one evening that started the wheels in motion. Jane happened to catch a glimpse of the sweet, gentle-looking little guy during a "Pet of the Week" segment on TV, and it was as if a lightning bolt struck. "I will never forget that face on TV," she says. It stopped her in her tracks. There was something about the puppy that touched her, an instant connection.

Now she was a woman with a mission. So determined was she that the next morning, Jane and her husband Jay found themselves standing outside the city's Animal Care and Control office, waiting for the doors to open. It was a frigid February day, and Jay had had enough. He went back to sit in the car. Not Jane. "I wanted to be the first one at the door," she says. When another gentleman came and stood outside the locked doors, Jane grilled him to make sure he wasn't coming to get last night's TV dog.

It was an odd time in life for the dog urge to strike. The Jorgensens hadn't been looking for a dog. Their oldest child, Ben, was getting ready to go off to college. Their daughter Molly was an active high school student. They already had a dog named Indy, who was getting up in years. Yet there was no doubt in Jane's mind that this dog was supposed to come home with her. "It was meant to be," she says.

They named him Teddy, and typical for a Hound, he is gentle and easy-going, a calming influence in the Jorgensen's busy lives. Teddy may be able to thank the wonders of broadcasting for his new family, but the Jorgensens thank Teddy for the happiness he has brought to them. Impulsive though it was, no one in the family regrets the decision to adopt Teddy. To this day, Jane wonders, "Who could drop off this dog? He's just so dear."

Teddy holds the attention of owners Molly, Jay and Jane Jorgensen.

REVEREND RALPH

You won't hear him preaching from the pulpit. In fact, you couldn't even see him if he got behind a pulpit. But the Reverend Ralph Van Leeper III commands an audience, all the same. That's because the "reverend" in question isn't a man, but a seven-and-a-half year old Dachshund, and he holds court several times a week at Oz Flowers and Gifts. His owner, Rhonda Leeper, is also the manager of the store. She says Reverend Ralph has become a fixture at Oz.

Customers seek him the moment they come in, and Reverend Ralph is more than willing to step right into the spotlight. Thanks to the tuxedo shop located near Oz, Reverend Ralph greets his fans in a variety of snappy outfits. "They're always bringing him different ties," says Rhonda, rolling her eyes.

Rhonda's mother surprised her with Reverend Ralph one weekend, after Rhonda had returned from a trip with her daughters. Rhonda and her ex-husband had shared custody of a Labrador Retriever named Odie they owned during their marriage, but Rhonda says it was always hard to say goodbye to Odie after his weekly visitation. So her mother decided to take action. She felt Rhonda needed her own canine companion, and the tiny Dachshund fit the bill. Rhonda named him Reverend Ralph because "he looks like he's preaching at you," she says. Later, when Rhonda's mom entered a nursing home, Reverend Ralph paid regular visits with Rhonda, and even went to the funeral home with her when her mother passed away. "He sat in my arms, he never moved," says Rhonda, "it was like he just knew."

Obviously, Rhonda's mom knew what she was doing when she bought Reverend Ralph. He is the perfect companion, and Rhonda will continue bringing the Reverend to the store, where he's a hit with patrons. Besides, laughs Rhonda, "he's too small to knock anything over."

Reverend Ralph shows his style with owner Rhonda Leeper.

... AND THEY ALL LIVED HAPPILY EVER AFTER

Every book needs a great ending. This final chapter is courtesy of Lori Hunt, who took all the photographs for this book. After shooting almost two dozen dog owners with their beloved pets, the final picture she got to take was of her own children - with their brand new dog, Cosmo!

Cosmo, a Shih Tzu puppy, was actually acquired right after what was supposed to be the book's last shoot. Lori had just photographed the Warner family with their dog Asta, and the enthusiasm of all these dog lovers was apparently too much to resist. The Hunts had been talking about getting a dog, so instead of driving straight home after the Warner's photo session, Lori took a little detour, and wound up buying Cosmo!

That was just fine with her two sons, thirteen-year-old Daniel and ten-year-old Weston, who welcomed the tiny dog with open arms. Even husband Darren was bowled over by Cosmo. "We are really enjoying him," says Lori, who admits Cosmo has changed life in the Hunt household, but in a good way. "The kids are just wild about him," she says. It is a sentiment to which all the dog owners who have been in front of her lens can relate. To the entire Hunt family - welcome to the club!

Daniel and Weston Hunt couldn't be happier with new dog Cosmo!

In Memoriam

*In loving memory of those pets who passed away
during the completion of this book:*

James, owned by Sandi Kemmish

Michie, owned by Jill Burnett

Minnie, owned by Karen Springer

*You think dogs will not be in heaven?
I tell you, they will be there long before any of us.*

Robert Louis Stevenson

No man can be condemned for owning a dog.
As long as he has a dog, he has a friend;
and the poorer he gets, the better friend he has.

Will Rogers